derek jarman's garden

with photographs by howard sooley

150 illustrations, 90 in colour

Photographs © 1995 Howard Sooley
Text © 1995 Estate of Derek Jarman

British Library Cataloguing-in-Publication Data
A catalogue record for this book is available from the British library

ISBN 0-500-01656-9

Printed and bound in Singapore by C.S. Graphics

preface

In 1986, on a springtime afternoon drive through Kent, searching for a bluebell wood to Super-8 for the film which would become The Garden, *Derek suggested eating at the Pilot Inn, Dungeness – renowned for serving 'Simply the finest fish and chips in all England'.*

Charmed by the landscape, we decided to visit the old lighthouse. Derek said: 'There's a beautiful fisherman's cottage here, and if ever it was for sale, I think I'd buy it.' As we neared the cottage, black varnished with bright yellow window frames, we saw the green-and-white 'For Sale' sign – the improbability of it made the purchase inescapable.

The garden started accidentally: a sea-worn driftwood staff topped with a knuckle of beachcombed bone was used to stake a transplanted dog rose, and an elongated lowtide flint protected a seedling seakale from careless feet. Over the coming year more beachcombed treasures were added.

Howard arrived at Prospect Cottage to photograph Derek in 1991. He was a keen plantsman and gave up London weekends to chauffeur Derek – via the nurseries of the south of England – to Prospect Cottage. With his collaboration the garden entered its second phase: the unexpected successes of new plants and bulbs, flint and scallop-shell edged beds, honey bees enclosed in a raised herb bed, and more seashore-rusted metal and wind-twisted wood.

Slowly the garden acquired a new meaning – the plants struggling against biting winds and Death Valley sun merged with Derek's struggle with illness, then contrasted with it, as the flowers blossomed while Derek faded.

Howard photographed the garden from his first visit. Derek's writing was completed in the last year of his life: on trips to the garden; in St Bartholomew's Hospital; and on a final holiday, to look at Monet's garden at Giverny.

Dungeness is a magical location. When you visit, tread softly, for many choose to live here for the solitude and silence that once attracted Derek, and now holds me.

Keith Collins (HB)

Prospect Cottage
Garden book

weve been hunting all year
old secateurs for Howard and to im
none I found mine in a flea market
from Florence.

So maybe we'll find his on
our trip to France ~ gardeners
~~develope a~~ and passion ~~for~~ toryate about
rakes and hoes. ive had my
hoe cast in bronze and it sits
on the window at phoenix house
one of the few objects that has passed
the H.B. test ~ my earliest memories
are of the old lawn mower with which

We've been hunting all year for old secateurs for Howard and found none. I found mine in a flea-market in Florence, so maybe we'll find his on our trip to France. Gardeners are passionate about rakes and hoes. I've had my hoe cast in bronze and it sits on the windowsill at Phoenix House, one of the few objects that has passed the HB test.

My earliest memories are of the old lawn-mower with which we laboured to cut the grass. I am so glad there are no lawns in Dungeness. The worst lawns, and for that matter the ugliest gardens, are along the coast in Bexhill – in Close and Crescent. These are the 'gardens' that would give Gertrude Jekyll a heart attack or turn her in her grave. Lawns, it seems to me, are against nature, barren and often threadbare – the enemy of a good garden. For the same trouble as mowing, you could have a year's vegetables: runner beans, cauliflowers and cabbages, mixed with pinks and peonies, shirley poppies and delphiniums; wouldn't that beautify the land and save us from the garden terrorism that prevails?

My first garden tool was a little trowel with which I kept the flowerbeds in front of the Nissen hut in order. When I left home in 1960 my parents kept my spades and rakes for me and after my father died I stored them behind a chest in my flat in London.

My precious hoe is worn down by work, its head held to the shaft by three rusty nails. The rake is even nearer my heart because its shaft broke and I put the whole thing in the bonfire to clean out the wood and replaced it with a very beautiful piece of driftwood.

Rake, hoe, shovel and trowel are the most useful tools here, and the secateurs to clip back the santolinas; spades and forks are of little use, except for shifting manure. The wood of the tools is polished by my hand; the rake, which is used most often, glitters a dull pewter.

There is a shop in Appledore which has wonderful garden tools and is very inexpensive. I bought a utility spade there, with its ace-of-spades shape, for £7. Unlike woodworking tools, there isn't yet a market in garden tools, which are objects of both practicality and great beauty.

Old tools serve as garden sculpture
Opposite: Cotton lavender

I was always a passionate gardener –
flowers sparkled in my childhood as they do in
a medieval manuscript. I remember daisies –
white and red – daisy chains on the lawn,
fortresses of grass clippings, and of course the
exquisite overgrown garden of Villa Zuassa, by
Lake Maggiore, where in April 1946 my parents
gave me my first grown-up book: *Beautiful Flowers
and How to Grow Them.* The garden cascaded down
to the lake, its paths banked by huge camellias.
The beds were full of fiery scarlet pelargoniums –
the scent of red. By the shore, lizards ran over
a stone monument.

There were enormous pumpkins, and mulberry
trees to feed the silkworms belonging to the little
lady in black who lived in the lodge. The flowers
in the beds along the rose pergola – lupins,
peonies and shirley poppies – bloomed under the
showers of petals from the pink roses. The heady
scent of privet and lime drifted into the walled
garden.

I came home to my parents' married quarters
and planted a purple iris. My father capitalized on
my interest and was happy to let me mow the
lawn, but my childhood passion was put to an
end when I moved up to London at eighteen.

*Opposite: Indigenous flowers by
the roadside: poppies and viper's
bugloss*

*Below: At the back of the
garden, showing the watertank
with poppies at base and with
flints and lichen-covered stones
on top. The power station is
visible in the background*

When I came to Dungeness in the
mid-eighties, I had no thought of building a
garden. It looked impossible: shingle with no soil
supported a sparse vegetation. Outside the front
door a bed had been built – a rockery of broken
bricks and concrete: it fitted in well. One day,
walking on the beach at low tide, I noticed a
magnificent flint. I brought it back and pulled
out one of the bricks. Soon I had replaced all the
rubble with flints. They were hard to find, but
after a storm a few more would appear. The bed
looked great, like dragon's teeth – white and
grey. My journey to the sea each morning had
purpose.

I decided to stop there; after all, the bleakness
of Prospect Cottage was what had made me fall
in love with it. At the back I planted a dog rose.
Then I found a curious piece of driftwood and
used this, and one of the necklaces of holey
stones that I hung on the wall, to stake the rose.
The garden had begun.

I saw it as a therapy and a pharmacopoeia.
I collected more driftwood and stones and put
them in. I dug small holes – almost impossible,
as the shingle rolled back so that two spadefuls
became one – and filled them with manure from

Right: In back garden

the farm up the road. The plants were just plonked
in and left to take their chances in the winds of
Dungeness. The easterlies are the worst; they bring
salt spray which burns everything. The westerlies only
give a battering. We have the strongest sunlight, the
lowest rainfall, and two less weeks of frost than the
rest of the U.K. Dungeness is set apart, at 'the fifth
quarter', the end of the globe; it is the largest shingle
formation, with Cape Canaveral, in the world.

Sea kale, *Crambe maritima*, is the Ness's most distinguished plant. There are more of them here than anywhere in England – they come up between the boats. *Crambe* are edible, but a radiologist told me that they accumulate radioactivity from the nuclear power station more than any other plant.

They die away completely in winter, just a bud on the corky stem. In March they start to sprout – the first sign of spring. The leaves are an inky

Sea kale (Crambe maritima) *in spring*

purple which looks fine in the ochre pink pebbles, but they rapidly lose the purple and become a glaucous blue-green.

Then buds appear; by May these turn into sprays of white flowers with little yellow centres – they have a heavy, honey scent which blows across the Ness. The flowers then turn into seeds – which look like a thousand peas. They lose their green and become the colour of bone. At this stage they are at their most beautiful – sprays of pale ochre, several thousand seeds on each plant. The autumn winds return, the leaves rot at the

Opposite
Above: Sea kale in seed
Below: Sea kale in flower

Below: Dried sea kale

base, dry out and blow away; by November the *Crambe* has completely disappeared.

Year after year they come back – some of the plants must be fifty years old. In the humus that collects around them other plants spring up, but the *Crambes* hold sway. Caterpillars give up on them – they are too tough; a snail or two might bite a hole, but on the whole they are left alone. They look their best in sunlight after rain as the leaves are designed to catch the rain and feed it to the centre of the plant; the beads of water glittering on the plant are an ecstasy.

They survive in this terrain because they have roots at least twenty feet long – I discovered this after a storm washed the shingle away, exposing them.

Gertrude Jekyll's observations about the use of
colour in gardens are nowhere more apposite than
here. Also, certain plants do not fit in – daffodils in
the shingle are the most surreal. Actually, the
delicate early daffodil fares best. King Alfreds look
like mutton dressed as lamb – I have a clump that
I'm going to pull out any day. White pinks (like Mrs
Sinkins), the wild red poppies which splash the
Ness with colour, and the sky blue cornflower
which comes up in every corner, look best. Dog
roses grow here, bleach bone and skeletal.

'When gorse ceases flowering, kissing goes out the window.'

The gorse is wonderful in the winter, splashes the garden in March with its glorious yellow. I have planted two circles of it at each side of the house, with baulks of timber at the centre. It's a chancy business, as the first year's cuttings which I planted out disappeared overnight. Rabbits have a passion for gorse, and further across the shingle they have clipped them into cones – gorse makes a good topiary.

My own circles are just begun. I have protected them with driftwood cones which I invented to keep the rabbits at bay – successfully. The circles

21

should look magnificent in a few years. Gorse is not long-lived, but it is easily replaced and its golden flowers put the winter gloom to fright.

It's one of our most neglected shrubs and would make a great hedge around a garden, definitely one to deter the unwanted. I would have made a gorse hedge here, but the charm of Dungeness is that it has no fences – to build one would go against the grain.

Behind the gorse I have a stand of prostrate blackthorn. These grow almost flat over the Ness but mine are a couple of feet tall. Last year they waged an unequal battle against the browntail moth – a rarity, but unfortunately quite common here. It's a furry brown thing that it's not sensible to touch, which hides itself in fortress cocoons from which it emerges like a hungry army in spring. It has the unfortunate effect of poisoning the plants it eats – it punched holes in my dog roses. Normally it just eats the sloe, but it gobbled that up and moved on. There are only a few snow-like sloe flowers this year, so the purple fruit which makes the best gin will be thin on the ground.

Opposite: Sedum
Below: Gorse

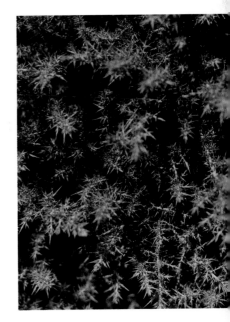

The stones, especially the circles, remind me of dolmens, standing stones. They have the same mysterious power to attract. After I had finished the rockery and the last brick was lobbed into the sea, I built the stone circle to the left as you stand in front of the cottage – it is about five feet in diameter and is composed of dragon-toothed flints, sea-ground bricks for a splash of colour and stones and shells of interest. It took the best part of winter to construct it, though I was helped by an American plumber's bag which enabled me to bring half a dozen stones in one trip.

The circle gave the key to the formal front garden. Soon another, to the right of the house, was constructed, mirroring the original. This was followed by the oblong bed in the centre, filled with white pebbles, with a central circle of red and grey stones.

There are three geometric shapes as you approach the front door: the central oblong bed is preceded by a circular bed. It has grey upright flints, an annulus of grey pebbles, a second circle of flints which lie flat, then fine shingle with a pruned-back elder planted at the centre.

Nearer the house a circle of salvia now hides the outermost circle of stones, then comes a ring of alternating flints and driftwood sticks; fine gravel and pebbles give way to a central circle of blue-grey pebbles with a large central upright flint; in this central blue circle two blue-flowered lavenders have self-sown.

The back of the garden is random, the front formal.

Left: Front of Prospect Cottage. In the foreground is a circle of flints and shingle, with a round clump of elder in the centre

Below: Cistus grows at the foot of a driftwood sculpture

Elder is perhaps the most neglected hedgerow plant, though it is the source of elderflower wine, of cordial, and also of an excellent pudding – the flowers deep-fried in batter and sprinkled with sugar are a great delicacy. In the hedgerow elder grow leggy, but here, hugged into themselves as protection from the sun and wind, they become a shrub, six feet at most, with a beautiful shape made of a thousand small branches.

They are out early, the first sprinkling of green that with the *Crambe* brings in the spring, though these premature young leaves are burnt black when the easterly comes. Besides the one at the front I have three at the back, one of which, the second plant I put in, is now three foot high and will bloom this year. Elders keep witches at bay, and any old cottage garden that has not been modernized will have one growing alongside the house. The white flowers turn to purple berries; the plant keeps its bone-coloured dead branches and looks even more attractive. Roses are the same – bushes with dead branches, pink-grey, swaying in the wind.

The perennial pea, the sea pea, grows wild here – the pinky-purple one that you will know. The other is pink and green, like an orchid.

Rear views of Prospect Cottage

Above: Giant sea kale (Crambe cordifolia) *in flower outside the kitchen door*

Dungeness has its own flora – chiefly
marked out by stands of deep green broom. This is
covered with golden flowers which blaze throughout
June. Then some plants die and the rest of them
wait for the easterlies to burn them black.

I have two large stands at the back – they protect
the wild flowers like fennel and the stinking hawks-
beard that has been reintroduced to the Ness by the
ecology department of Sussex University. Most of
the hawks-beard has been eaten by the rabbits,
though some of the plants rotted in the little squares
that the ecologists cut out to plant them in. Next
door they seem to have fared better – I have only
one plant left.

Above and opposite: Fennel,
and poppy seed-heads

My garden is ecologically sound, though work of any kind disrupts the existing terrain. Dungeness is an SSSI (Site of Special Scientific Interest), so there are restrictions on what plants can be grown – though to extend this to the fishermen's gardens seems a little hard.

In any case, so many weeds are spectacular flowers: the white campion, mallow, rest-harrow and scabious look wonderful. Introducing these local flowers into the garden makes a little wilderness at the heart of paradise. And there can be no complaints about my flint garden – it spoilt nothing. It was built over the drive of the old cottage.

The dog roses are the joy of the copse by the lakes. Once, when I was transplanting a small seedling to the garden, I was assaulted by an ecological puritan from Canterbury.

'Do you realize you could be doing damage?'

'Yes,' I said.

'Well why are you planting that rose?'

'It's a Dungeness plant. If the world stopped still and humanity ceased, who could tell if it had been planted by me or by a bird?'

He drove off.

Dungeness has a host of lichens, some of them very rare. There are mosses too: reindeer moss, vivid bright-green mosses, and dodder, with its pink flowers – a muted rainbow. To walk across this velvet carpet after rain is one of the pleasures of the area.

The wood holds many surprises: a fig, a dwarf pear, ragged robin, cuckoo-pint, along with sallow, roses and escaped periwinkle, teazle and laceflower.

In the copse are two lakes, formed by the sea 10,000 years ago. They are fringed with yellow irises and wild mint. There are swans, ducks, flocks of greenfinches, and goldfinches as well. Dungeness is full of twitchers with binoculars, the dirty old men of the avian world:

'Is that a Kentish plover or the Lydd eagle?'

We have plenty of kestrels and the year before last black and white hobbies, the most agile and beautiful birds I have ever seen. And, of course, Sylvia's crow, Jet, rescued and become so tame that he was in the kitchen like a flash, croaking and casting his eye over glittering objects – stealing teaspoons, silver foil and all my clothes pegs, hiding them in the santolina and the helichrysum.

Once a robin came, and also a wren, but crows and seagulls rule here.

Howard Sooley is like a giraffe, a giraffe
that has stared a long time at a photo of Virginia
Woolf; he possesses the calm and sweetness of
that miraculous beast. When he takes a photo he
stands like a T that has lost half an arm; he
smiles, clicks, mutters little words of
encouragement – more to himself or to the
garden – 'Ooh,' he says, 'that's nice.'

Howard is mauve, he dresses impeccably in
mauves, violets; he is the only man who can wear
purple, which he does infrequently and with
effect. He hails from Doncaster and has retained
a beautiful soft brogue. He is without ambition,
has the calm of a man who knows his worth, and
has a passion for plants. It is he who has
informed the second phase of building our

paradise, brought me to Elizabeth Strangman's
Hellebore Heaven, to Sempervivum Sam, and to the
most charming nursery in England – Madrona, up
the road in Lydd. He is known by the writer Beth
Chatto, and by Elizabeth Strangman. I must
introduce him to Christopher Lloyd.

At the moment Howard's garden is packaged and sent to his parents in the north while he finds a new home.

Howard came here to photograph me in 1991 and had more knowledge than I did of the plants in his backgrounds. He offered to drive me here a week later and arrived armed with a plant guide. Since I don't drive, Hellebore Heaven, the well-stocked garden centre at Bodiam and the nursery with the sinister name Starve Crow were all beyond my reach.

Howard also has a passion for garden tools, hence the secateurs.

He has delicate hands – no giraffe's hoofs these – that float in the air, and a charm with which he could have become the last of the Marx brothers.

He is always laughing, soft-spoken. I've never seen him gloomy; he holds that to himself, both girlfriend and garden gone. He is one of the most distinguished Englishmen that I have met and his portraits of me have changed the way I look. They are flattering but also revealing and have replaced the photos of 'Derek the black magician' that photographers caught like the measles in the early 1980s. He is the perfect man for the job, as he knows his plants as well as the sticks and stones.

*Front and rear views of
Prospect Cottage, showing
the formality of the front
garden and the informality
of the back*

The word paradise is derived from the ancient Persian – 'a green place'.

Paradise haunts gardens, and some gardens are paradises. Mine is one of them. Others are like bad children – spoilt by their parents, over-watered and covered with noxious chemicals. The only chemical I have used is against the slug which devours my *Crambe cordifolia*. I'm very selective – the *Crambe maritima* acts as a good slughouse and I like the look of them crawling across the sparkling leaves after a shower.

Other paradises: Christopher Lloyd's Great Dixter up the road. Gardens that deny paradise: Hidcote Manor, known to us as Hideouscote, which is so manicured that not one plant seems to touch its neighbour. The National Trust must have a central nursery as all their gardens look like that.

You won't find this in Great Dixter; it's shaggy. If a garden isn't shaggy, forget it.

The most amusing and surprising garden
I ever saw, the sister of Prospect Cottage, is in
Baku, Azerbaijan. The landscape there is pretty
much like Dungeness but it is black with oil
from the polluting oilfields; in the middle of the
grim housing blocks is a little circular walled
garden which an old power worker, avuncular,
smiling, looking much like Picasso, built as a
memorial for his daughter who had died in a
swimming accident.

He built maybe one hundred concrete
animals, exquisite leaping deer, leopards and
lions, as well as leafy bowers and a ziggurat with
a spiral staircase. This tower had a room with
windows in animal shapes, its floor strewn with
fine local carpets. Around the tower, in every
corner, is a practical vegetable garden, of which
he is very proud.

Before I left he said:

'You know the people in Moscow are mad.
I sent them a blueprint for an engine that
worked without all this black oil and they never
replied.'

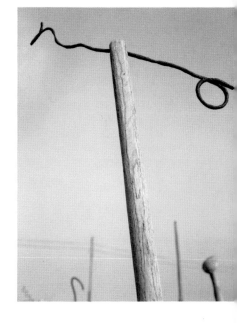

Sculptures made from tools and
found objects

Dungeness is at its best in the golden light of summer. The black house turns gold and casts a shadow that nearly touches the sea. The pale shingle reflects the light long after the sun has set behind the power station, turning the pink to bone. Twilight here is like no other. It lingers in a perfect calm. You feel as you stand here that tired time is having a snooze.

O Paradise, my garden dressed in light, you dissolve into the night.

Tomorrow morning at six a fox will be on the snoop and a little later when the day warms up a garden snake will be curled up by the compost heap. Once a hedgehog pulled up outside the front door, and a kestrel flew into a window with a terrible thump and lay stunned for a minute.

The sun is up, and the lizards that run hither and thither in the santolina and bask in the sun are out. There are more of them in my garden than anywhere else on the Ness and they love the scented shrubs. If I move a stone I'll find a small one underneath – so the stones come in handy.

The rabbits have gone – I'm happy about that, but welcome the hare that lops past. A hare is the queer animal of myth, and my, they go fast.

I have two friendly cats: a tortoiseshell pied who comes very infrequently and Sylvia's gorgeous Thomas, black as the cottage. Thomas marches past – a sergeant-major of cats. He is friendly but distant and so old even he can't remember. He searches for the mice which invade in the autumn, and he wears them so that it looks as if he had bagged Lord Kitchener's moustache – one less mouse to run up and down my dresser. I quite like the little black ones; the brown ones I catch in traps – sometimes six in one night. I have not seen any rats; they live on the fishheads by the boats.

Oh, those pesky browntail moths are munching again. I'm going to go to war. I expect they're highly protected but I'm going to shut my eyes to the slaughter. They're killing the prostrate blackthorn which is rarer than they are in these parts. I can hear the demons munching and the sloes screaming, 'Help!'.

Opposite: Front of Prospect Cottage

Below and following pages: Views at rear of cottage

45

At first, people thought I was building a garden for magical purposes — a white witch out to get the nuclear power station. It did have magic — the magic of surprise, the treasure hunt. A garden *is* a treasure hunt, the plants the paperchase.

I invest my stones with the power of those at Avebury. I have read all the mystical books about ley-lines and circles — I built the circles with this behind my mind. The circles make the garden perfect — in winter they take over from the flowers. There was magic and hard work in finding the coloured stones for the front: white, difficult; grey, less so; red, very rare.

Some of the flints are over a foot high: these are the central hub; some are grey, a very few white and a warm brown, the others mottled white and grey. The bricks, washed smooth by the tide, bring a jolly flash of red. The large circles are four feet in diameter and between the flint dolmens are shells and coloured stones from the beach. The stakes are head-high. I haven't named them, so they are difficult to identify; some have the holey stones made into necklaces, some have large single stones or bone caps; there's one twisted tangle of chain that has a lobster claw — that one *has* got a name: 'the snake'; there are wind chimes — two of

them with metal triangles to swing. There is a lantern, a crucifix and a verdigris trumpet.

Down the centre of the back garden is a rough spine which starts with three poles outside the kitchen window. Then there is a piece of maritime wood, like a gravestone, which is hugged by the silver-green santolina – silvery plants do well here. After that comes a purple sage which keeps its shape and what looks like a timber windowbox which is filled with special stones and metal, including a rusty boating hook. Then comes a cistus and another circle round a piece of driftwood; this last circle has green santolina (which has a delicious resinous smell) alternating with the grey – a vegetable harlequin. After that a yucca, whose white, bell-shaped flowers glisten in the autumn twilight. The santolina is not going to flower this year as I am trimming it into shape.

The edge of the garden starts with burgundy purple rugosa; next comes my enormous artichoke which towers over a bright green acanthus; then a gap to get through; then a perennial pea and lavender; then a peony; another gap; a rose which is swamped by marigolds and a magnificent horehound; two very special sages from Beth Chatto; irises; a drift of cornflower; more cistus and an endstop with a post and another harlequinade of santolina.

Such excitement – I found opium poppies growing wild in Greatstone, probably a Victorian escapee. The colour of an opium poppy is indescribable – pale white which shades to a delicate mauve. They have wonderful blue-green leaves, last a day, and then the seed heads ripen. Last year I found a lady picking them and I went spare – if it were polite to have hit her I would have done; instead, she got a string of abuse and I snatched her loot out of her hand.

These poppies, scattered around, have sprung up in corners. This year there are more of them than ever. I'm waiting for one to jump the boundary and seed itself all around like the fennel.

Opium poppies

After the sea kale, the second plant of the Ness is viper's bugloss. It's a plant well worth considering for an ordinary garden – here, of course, it pops up where it seeds itself. It usually has bright-blue flowers, though there are a few pink ones and last year I had a white, which surprised me. I christened it *Arvensis sooleyii*. This flower is the flower of twilight; it glows brighter and brighter as the light fails. Bees have a passion for it. It's slightly prickly to the touch – the leaves are covered in tiny spines – and has black, oddly shaped seeds in pods in clusters of four or five.

Above: Valerian
Opposite: Viper's bugloss

The valerian: the verges of the road along the Ness are pink and white with valerian in June. My own is just budding early in May. It doesn't last very long, but has a second flowering, particularly if you cut it back.

I have always loved this plant. It clung to the old stone walls of the manor at Curry Mallet which my father rented in the early fifties, and grew in the garden of the bomb-damaged house at the end of the road which the airman Johnny, my first love, took me to on his motorbike, with my hands in his trouser pockets – so valerian is a sexy plant for me.

53

My bees are in a hive protected by the vegetable and herb garden. The hive is made of railway sleepers in an oblong shape with the side missing to give them access.

The bees came as a gift from Mr Hart, from whom I bought my traditional WBC hive.

The bees emerge in January after a winter sleep; they are out in force today. I have never been stung by a bee, except one whom I inadvertently squashed. My hive is four storeys tall and produces pounds of honey as the Ness is never without flowers – in August they go for the woodsage, in

January the gorse. I don't think they bother to fly to the rape field four miles away in Lydd.

I leave them enough honey to winter and eat very little myself, give the rest away – Dungeness gold. I love to sit and watch them, their pollen sacs all different yellows. Last year I had two swarms, which I gave to a local beekeeper, Gary Scott, who came in yesterday as I've lost the strength to lift the combs. The bees of infinity, the golden swarm: it's sad when I lock them up for winter with a mouseguard, but they, and the snowdrops, herald the spring.

The vegetable and herb garden has thyme
and oregano, hyssop, lavender, rue, fennel and
rosemary, caraway, artemisia, pinks, a few sweet
peas, night-scented stock, rows of lamb's tongue,
purslane, peas, radish, onion, lettuce, spinach and
purple rocket.

The bed was built in December by Karl. Finely
graded topsoil was bought in from a local dealer
and then well dunged. Black polythene lining
keeps in the moisture. The first plants went in in
February and the seeds last week, in late April.
The seeds are up now and Howard is there with
the Phostrogen spray.

I can look at one plant for an hour, this
brings me great peace. I stand motionless and
stare. But mostly I'm bustling about. Today I'm
wearing a jellaba and look like a monk – a warm
jellaba keeps the heat in better than any coat.
I don't have gardening gear, usually wear what
I'm already wearing, plus gloves, and always a hat,
as the illness has made me very light-sensitive.

Watering in the seeds in the
vegetable and herb garden

On the path to the sea, the star-of-Bethlehem
grows wild on the verges next to the cabbages and
sweet peas. A couple of hundred yards along there is
an old gravel path which gives access to the boats.
Then there is a high bank which reveals itself as the
sea retreats, and sand flats as far as the eye can see,
reflecting the sky.

From the shingle little streams spring up and
carve water courses. There is never anybody on the

beach, though the fishermen are high above mending their nets. The only other human souls are the luggers and shrimpers in their yellow oilies with their huge triangular nets. It is a picture by Boudin, of isolation, of the vast forces of sky and sea.

At night the ships twinkle as they pass along the Channel; distant voyagers and sailors drop bottles with messages which I find as I walk along the shore. In the winter black cormorants bob in the waves, appearing and disappearing. On a sultry summer evening you can see the shadow of France. Over the way are the white cliffs of Dover which dazzle in a shaft of sun on a grey day – 'Earth hath not anything to show more fair.'

A ramble along the beach takes you past old boats rotting in the sun. Of the newer ones, the catamaran is the jazziest. It's a bit of a trudge. In the old days they wore backstays, pronounced 'baxters' – short wooden 'skis' strapped onto their shoes. Imagine Aggie-One-Tooth – who rang the alarm on a hand-bell; now they have a new lifeboat which is heaved across the sands by a caterpillar track after the maroons go off and shake the china.

The huts on the beach are rusted corrugated iron, the abandoned ones flap forlornly and are full of garden treasure. The roads up here are composed of rubble – even household rubbish. Two pits have been opened to try to stop the mess. The lone fishermen of the night are particularly to blame. And rubbish bins seem to have made the matter worse. Before, the people who cared took their rubbish home – now it is left to blow everywhere. But the rubble and brick and broken tiles do introduce some flowers. There is camomile, wild wallflowers and stock.

Here there are forty boats snuggling up and the heavenly sound of a thousand flags and pennants blowing in the wind. I wanted to buy the cream and red lifeboat station with its unfinished interior to make into a Dungeness museum, but it's slipped back into use – probably a better end.

The road bends round; on either side is a large purple vetch – almost a sweet pea. At the end of the road is a concrete PLUTO blockhouse – now a chapel open for Harvest Festival and Christmas Eve – where once the drowned were brought. Dungeness, where two seas meet, is a perilous place for ships. There are a hundred wrecks, including a German submarine.

Garden sculpture with cotton lavender

In the Second World War they thought the
Germans might land at Dungeness, so the area
was mined and anti-tank fencing put up. One day
I found one of the fence posts, its shaft curled
into loops for threading barbed wire, with one
end twisted into a giant corkscrew to penetrate
the shingle. Then I began to find them all over.
Turned upside-down and formed into pyramids,
they make good climbing frames for the plants.

Mine craters are rich in plantlife, which shows
that meddling with the landscape works. Mrs
Oiller, my neighbour, said that when they
destroyed the mines they bungled it and the whole
lot went off at once, blasting the windows, lifting
the roof and toppling chimneys. The explosion
broke her teacups, the handles and bottoms left
neatly on the hooks on the dresser.

Why have I escaped from the garden? Because
it has no fence or boundaries, so who can guess
where it ends?

My jolly friend and neighbour passes in his big
white Citroën. Derek is the *bon viveur* of the Ness,
a colour predictor for the fashion industry.
A refugee from Cape Town, with large owlish
glasses, he's started his own garden up the road
at Windshift – unkindly changed to Windshit.

Prospect Cottage is a beaut. I found it on a bluebell hunt with Tilda Swinton and HB seven years ago. The bluebells proved quite difficult to find, but we did manage to get wonderful fish and chips in a pub in Dungeness.

I had noticed the little fisherman's cottage, with its black varnish and yellow windows, before, when I was in Dungeness making two images in *The Last of England*. I had been struck by the area's otherworldly atmosphere – unlike any other place I had ever been – and the extraordinary light.

As we were driving around we passed the cottage and Tilda shouted:

'That one's for sale, let's stop.'

'No, go on.'

So we stopped, of course, and met Peggy, who had the voice of a male blues singer. She made us a cup of tea and charmed me into buying the place. She wanted to move quickly and so did I, but the leasehold was held by the Dungeness Estate, whose wheels seemed to have rusted. When they started to ask for references, I panicked – I suppose if I were to build a Howitzer I could hit Dungeness B. I had paranoid dreams of being vetted. Why was it taking so long? So I wrote to my friends Lord Sainsbury and Grey Gowrie to calm my fears and put my mind at rest. The letters and the keys came quickly. I bought the freehold and a little extra land for £750, a price I still think is a bargain.

Prospect Cottage was put up by a local builder in 1900, for the Richardsons – one of the leading fishing families. The present Mr Richardson, a kindly man, sells the best fish, fresh and local.

The house is a gem. It has four rooms off a central corridor and is lined with rich tongue and groove. It now has an extension built by Brian Clarke, a charming man who is a fine photographer. Brian is also putting in old-fashioned windows.

It was impossible to tell quite what a gem it was when I first saw it because the walls had disappeared in plasterboard, except for the room that is now the bedroom. But some weeks of HB stripping carpets and plasterboard revealed the wooden rooms. The corridor was painted sea-breeze blue and the front room a gloomy leaf green. The green is now gone, superseded by a canary yellow.

I replaced the stipple-glassed doors with wooden ones with small windows so the place is not claustrophobic – you can glance into a room past a closed door.

Opposite
Top: Early view of Prospect Cottage in 1986
Middle: Beginning the first stone circle
Below: Early stone circle

The furniture is simple, much of it created from bits and pieces from scrapyards and from beachcombings.

I have made many small sculptures, and two crosses dedicated to 'the fifth quarter'. There are poles with garlands of stones on the walls. There are also my landscapes, Robert Medley's great altarpiece from *Sebastiane* and an anti-communist oil that came from the Arbat in Moscow. In the kitchen is an old dresser and an antique larder in fine elm with gridded doors and slate shelves. There is not much else. The house is warm in the winter and cool in the heat.

Despite its sturdiness, it was badly shaken in the 1987 storm, which kept me awake in terror. We were at the storm's centre. The house swayed, and the old timbers, glued by a century's tar, cracked like rifles. The lights swung back and forth and dust blew in from forgotten crannies. In the morning – a grey morning with a mist of salt spray – I emerged to find my neighbour, Sylvia, who had came to see if I was all right. Buffeted this way and that, I made my way along the beach towards the shops. Iron-grey surfing rollers were marching along the shore, revealing canyons that stretched to the horizon, the tops of the waves blown in a

creamy spray – I kept well back. That morning the lights went out and it remained that way for the next five days. I sat at the kitchen table, shivering, with the nuclear power station a blaze of light.

The nuclear power station is a wonderment. At night it looks like a great liner or a small Manhattan ablaze with a thousand lights of different colours. A mysterious shadow surrounds it that makes it possible for the stars still to glow in a clear summer sky. I walk down to the beach with that slight insecurity you feel when you can hear the sea but

Inside the cottage
Above and opposite top: Views of study
Opposite below: Assemblage on the bedroom wall

not see it, a feeling I experienced dramatically, not here, but under the craggy battlements of Bamburgh castle when we went there to film *The Tempest*. It was pitch black and snow fell in huge white flakes, spectral white. Here, I walk out to the sea in the dark with Tilda and we discover that handfuls of flints thrown to the ground produce a shower of sparks.

Prospect has been re-tarred; it's shining and will remain so till the elements dull it. The west wall is the worst, sun and driving wet westerlies flake the paint in a year, so it has to be painted continuously to keep the timbers in shape. Painting the house with tar varnish takes a day. Brian does it – though the roof is perilous and the tar slightly toxic if it's blown on the skin. HB finds it rather lethal, though the resinous smell that informs the whole house is very pleasant.

An outside staircase leads to an attic which used to hold the nets and cork floats. It is the length and breadth of the house but you have to be careful not to knock your head – it's fine for storage. There is a good view from the corrugated roof.

The windows are painted the cheery yellow that they were when we found it.

Both kinds of sea kale are magical, the *cordifolia* extraordinary, with flowers eight foot high.

Helichrysum, in which the lizards dance, is the backbone of the garden, both in the formal garden at the front and at the back. It just needs the flowers trimmed in August and requires no other attention. Cuttings are easy – I gave Derek Ball five yesterday.

Stone and wood sculptures
Opposite: Curry plant

My paradise at the fifth quarter looks better every year.

Under this blue sky
my clock-faced flowerbeds
reflect the orb of the sun.
They guard its rising
and mark its setting
in the western land.
They never sleep.

Lying awake under the starry constellations,
they listen to the music of time,
great ancestral voices,
Henge and Dolmen.
They chuckle, yes, they chuckle
and gossip.
The wise wren,
head cocked,
listens to them.
Fools sing life in an empty song
quickly lost in the wind,
insignificant.
How wrong.
Though the watch-spring breaks,
the batteries dry on the digits,
the sands of time never run dry:
they defy dread death.
I stand with my camera,
the film unwinding.
Is there nothing but mortality?
The rushes are quickly over,
I'm there with a second chance.
Time leaks
as the twelve apostles dance.

Opposite below:
Cardoon, helichrysum,
cotton lavender

My friend Howard Brookner dies in New York.
A letter falls through the door.
Words forget their sweet meaning,
drowned by time,
no one remembers the old story.
How can anything endure
the terrible rising of the sun,
the death of a thousand summers?
I sit here immobile,
the winter sun luminous
across the darkening waves,
your dreaming laughter
lost in the wind.
The heavens have stolen your smile,
the closed gates rust,
the rainbow is broken.
All our memories —
the wild night fucking you
on the floor of Heaven —
all our memories are wasted.
Salt tears wound my blinded eyes
as I write this,
fires stoked by strangers
consume your heart.
I stumble through the day of your passion.

Did you imagine one day the sun would not rise,

that I would be left

to bear witness to our friendship?

'Our names will be forgotten in time,

no one will remember our works.

Our life will pass away like traces of a cloud

and be scattered like mist

that is chased by the rays of the sun

and overcome by its heat.

For our lifetime is the passing of a shadow

and will run like sparks through the stubble.'

No dragons will spring from these circles,
these stones will not dance or clap hands
at the solstice.
Beached on the shingle,
they lock up their memories,
standing like sentinels.
Rolled by the sea down the centuries,
they wait for the great tide
that will come a second time,
calling them back to the depths,
where the salt sea will unlock their silence.
They'll talk to strange creatures
of their time here,
telling them how
the postman came up the path with your letter,
how I couldn't conceal my happiness
and walked backwards and forwards, skipping,
and when you came, we set off under a full moon
to watch the patient fishermen
throwing handfuls of pebbles in showers of sparks
under the starlit sky,
your green eyes lit by the beam of the lighthouse
every ten seconds,
a smile, a wink,
green-eyes,
holding hands.

I walk in this garden
holding the hands of dead friends.
Old age came quickly for my frosted generation,
cold, cold, cold, they died so silently.
Did the forgotten generations scream
or go full of resignation,
quietly protesting innocence?
I have no words,
my shaking hand cannot express my fury.
Cold, cold, cold, they died so silently.

Linked hands at 4 a.m.,
deep under the city you slept on,
never heard the sweet flesh song.
Cold, cold, cold, they died so silently.

Matthew fucked Mark fucked Luke fucked John
who lay on the bed that I lie on,
touch fingers again as you sing this song.
Cold, cold, cold, we die so silently.

My gilly flowers, roses, violets blue,
sweet garden of vanished pleasures,
Please come back next year.
Cold, cold, cold, I die so silently.

Goodnight boys, goodnight Johnny,
Goodnight, goodnight.

Opposite: Snowdrop
Below: Narcissus

Here at the sea's edge
I have planted my dragon-toothed garden
to defend the porch,
steadfast warriors
against those who protest their impropriety
even to the end of the world.
A fathomless lethargy has swallowed me,
great waves of doubt broken me,
all my thoughts washed away.
The storms have blown salt tears,
burning my garden,
Gethsemane and Eden.

Acanthus

The shivering cold continues.
The frozen larks creep through the shingle.
I catch my breath as the light fades:
death comes even for stones.
If I could just pull back the curtain…

Deep solemn waters
wash the dark shingle,
where pearl fishers
embrace
amphorae,
spilling gold.
And on the seabed,
in the shadows
of the billowing sails
of forgotten ships,
tossed by the mournful winds of the deep,
lost boys
sleep forever
in a dear embrace,
salt lips touching.
In submarine gardens,
cool marble arms embrace.
The waters fan
your antique smile,
deep love
drifting forever on the tide.

A cold, grey day. I write these poems, and while the poems form the rain blows in.

Slowly the puddles gather at the roadside. Then, as the day draws to a close, sunlight floods the Ness and the wet shingle glistens like pearls of Vermeer light.

The garden was made into an AIDS-related film but AIDS was too vast a subject to 'film'. All the art failed. It was well-intentioned but decorative – the graffiti artist Keith Haring raised consciousness and did much good but failed to turn the tragedy beyond the domestic.

The old stuff, like the *War Requiem*, still brought tears in parallel lines.

When the AIDS quilt came to Edinburgh during the film festival, I attended just out of duty. I could see it was an emotional work, it got the heartstrings. But when the panels were unveiled a truly awful ceremony took place, in which a group of what looked like refrigerated karate experts, all dressed in white, turned and chanted some mumbo jumbo – horrible, quasi-religious, false. I shall haunt anyone who ever makes a panel for me.

Those pesky little caterpillars of the browntail turn into little moths, white as snow and downy, but don't touch because they keep the poison that kills the plant in their gobby jaws. The moths don't seem to fly, but sit in the sunlight waiting for an unwary bird; the birds have learnt their lesson long ago and pass by. Today there are so many of these moths on the Ness, some bugloss plants have twenty or more clinging to them. They drift in waves over the sea, falling into the garden, a bridal confetti dancing in the sunlight.

Below: Rubber glove and stone

I sit reading on Güta's old garden bench, which welcomed me in past summers, when as a teenager I painted in her attic.

Güta was not an expert gardener but she did have an interest in plants, particularly the huge clumps of white and yellow iris that came up in the wilderness beyond her ruined tennis court. Donald, her husband, was actually in charge and grew all their houseplants in a greenhouse next to an apple tree I had planted.

Güta wore miner's kneecaps – a most sensible idea that I haven't seen anywhere since. Nut brown, wrinkled, with her light Danish accent, she was descended from the mistress of an eighteenth-

Opposite: Iris

Below: Derek Jarman revisiting his parents' house at Northwood, Middlesex, in his lapel a piece of wisteria from a plant he put in himself at the age of 16

century king. She possessed a necklace of
polished, but uncut, diamonds – one of the most
beautiful pieces of jewelry I ever saw.

She had been in the England fencing team, so
she sat straight-backed at the Christmas table,
jewels sparkling, like the tree ablaze with candles
whose light shimmered in the night.

Later, when she was very ill, my sister and
I went to visit her. The bench was outside, on the
porch. We took tea with Güta, who was
bedridden, propped on her great walnut bed. My
sister crossed the abandoned garden like a silent

Below from the left:
Burnt driftwood, cork floats,
driftwood, bucket handle

will-o'-the-wisp in her wedding dress, to show it off
to Güta, who was too unwell to attend the wedding.

After Güta died, and the bulldozers came,
I rescued the forgotten bench. Some years ago I had
the ruined parts replaced and a visiting antique
dealer said:

'My God, that's a rarity.'

'What?'

'The bench. It's eighteenth century, built for
a lady with a pannier.'

You can see my bench in Gainsborough's *Mr and
Mrs Andrews.*

I solved the rose problem: the plants I put
in never grew – they remain just a foot high. But
then, when Brian built my extension, it threw up
a lot of shingle and I built a bank beyond the white
rugosa. Immediately the roses improved, because
the bank caught a leeward damp. I've replanted all
of them alongside the drainpipes and they are as
green and healthy as can be.

There are three shingle mounds, all very carefully
placed. The first was here when I came; it has
a dog rose growing on it and a new broom at its
side, as well as vetch, and what I call clover –
grass pompoms that dance in the wind. The dry
grasses also do this and seem to catch fire in the
setting sun.

I was frightened of dandelions as a child.

The thrift is out, one of the wonderful wild
plants that has been embraced by the garden. Over
the other side of the nuclear station it carpets the
landscape; I bought one at Joanna's wild plant
nursery, and my one plant, with its bobbing pink
heads, is now fifty. It's going to leap about: it will
soon be across the road.

Allium

The flowerbeds' planting looks like this:

Left bed as you face the sea:
Lovage, which shoots up with its pale green leaves,
iris, cistus and chicory (which with the cornflower
has the bluest flowers), a verbena, rosemary, cistus,
wallflower, artemisia, santolina, wallflower, day lily,
two Mrs Sinkins pinks, the whole fringed by
sedum.

The right-hand bed:
Santolina, Mrs Sinkins pinks, fennel, restharrow,
wallflower, scabious, artichoke, more Mrs Sinkins,
small red rose, white perfumed sweet pea and rue –
which turns into a tight rue football.

The circular bed beyond:
Origanum, marigold, teazle, Mrs Sinkins pinks,
cabbage and wallflower.

The right side of the house:
Lavatera, evening primrose, foxglove, and other
Ness flora, including anchusa.

The second circular bed:
Comfrey, cornflowers, pinks, two small santolinas,
sage and geranium. It's a bit of a tangle, with a
broad-leafed parsley, which I will move,

Clockwise, from top left:
Hyacinth, cornflowers,
borage, sage

helichrysum and santolina, buttercups, roses,
Crambe maritima, grey-blue moss and sea-green pea.

Along the roads:
An exquisite white mallow (I call it 'angels
dancing'), the bright blue cousin of the viper's
bugloss, anchusa, rue, marigolds, a periwinkle –
this one variegated and covered with blue – rue
and a sage.

Over the road we have:
White campion, anchusa, thistle, sloes, horehound,
marigold, artichoke and helichrysum, foxglove,
sage and a pink.

Opposite: California poppies,
with sea kale (Crambe
maritima) *in background*

Below: Marigolds

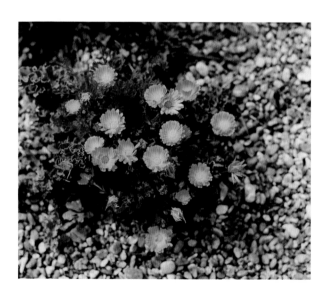

You see it is rather a wild garden; I really recommend this – out with those lawns and in with the stinging nettles and kerbside flowers: bluebells, pinks, purple orchids, drifts of buttercups – subtlety to the eye. (I don't see anything like this as I go about, just a desert of fuchsias, awful in July.) I would like anyone who reads my book to try this wildness in a corner. It will bring you much happiness.

I'm going to make some new chairs this summer, which I'm covering with driftwood.

Back to the butterflies. There are peacocks, tortoiseshells, painted ladies, and red admirals that come in packs – some are so tame they land on your fingers and you sit there, breathless. Then they're off, flying so fast around the house that you could almost miss them. Meadow-browns flutter, pushed this way and that in the grasses, and the blue, the blue butterfly . . .

Honesty

Lizards you are bent not straight.

Lizzy the lezzy

is quite the best,

she's made the mat

a little nest,

she's the sleekest lizard

of the lot,

curled in the sun

like a sleepy pussy

all yellow and green,

she's the best the HB's seen.

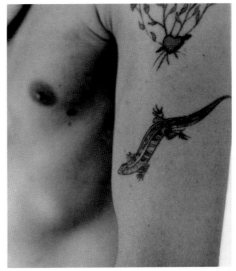

Sticks and stones may break your bones but words can never hurt you.

Opposite: Horehound
Below: Corkscrew fence posts

The garden is full of metal: rusty metal corkscrew clumps, anchors from the beach, twisted metal, an old table-top with a hole for the umbrella, an old window, chains which form circles round the plants. All this disappears in the burgeoning spring. The twisted grimace of the wartime mines, an arch, a hook, a plummet, a line, a shellcase – warlike once; a chain that has rusted to form a snake by the front door, more chimes made of triangles of rusty iron; all this – and the float that looks like an exotic fruit – introduces a warm brown which contrasts nicely with the shingle.

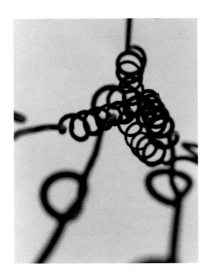

Opposite: At rear of cottage

Below left: At the seashore
Centre: Floats in the garden
Right: Upturned groyne

Along the front of the house are other 'sculptures' – a fine old box filled with cork floats. These floats are also made into necklaces which hang round the two old silver-grey chairs. On one of them my neighbour Brian Yale has inscribed on a slate:

> To see the world
>
> In a grain of sand
>
> And heaven in
>
> A flower

It would be great to invite Mr Blake and his lady wife to an Adam and Eve tea. I suppose I would be the old serpent who packed them off.

On the other side are two spectacular flints that I found while filming *War Requiem*. There's another on the exquisite upturned water tank which also has a stone from the beach covered with orange lichen.

Above: Helleborus orientalis *hybrids*
Opposite: Planting a hellebore

Above: Fishermen's huts by the sea

The night comes, the shingle dissolves in the dark. The stars are out and the great liner of Dungeness B twinkles on the horizon. Dawn can be a miracle, the sun floating up from the sea and slowly crossing the garden. As it passes it can laugh with John Donne, whose poem fills the southern wall of the house, before finally setting behind Lydd church.

Busie old foole, unruly Sunne,
why dost thou thus,

The Sunne Rising

Busie old foole, unruly Sunne,

Why dost thou thus,

Through windowes, and through curtaines call on us?

Must to thy motions lovers' seasons run?

Sawcy pedantique wretch, goe chide

Late schoole boyes and sowre prentices,

Goe tell Court-huntsmen, that the King will ride,

Call countrey ants to harvest offices;

Love, all alike, no season knowes, nor clyme,

Nor houres, dayes, moneths, which are the rags of time....

Thou sunne art halfe as happy as wee,

In that the world's contracted thus.

Thine age askes ease, and since thy duties bee

To warme the world, that's done in warming us.

Shine here to us, and thou art every where;

This bed thy centre is, these walls thy spheare.

Above right: Peter, putting up
'The Sunne Rising' on the side of
the cottage

The moon is even more spectacular. The sunset turns the seashore into a rosy mirror, with streaks of pink cloud. Then the moon comes, and casts a silver path across the waves, a shimmering carpet for the stars. Dungeness, Dungeness, your beauty is the best, forget the hills and valleys.

This landscape is like the face you overlook, the face of an angel with a naughty smile. There is very little to interrupt you here, just the wind, which, like the mistral, can drive you slightly mad.

The sea cadets pass, singing a shanty; the postman arrives with a smile and a huge pile of letters, from every corner of the globe, often addressed just to: Derek of Dungeness, wishing me well and happy, which I am. These years have been the most extraordinary, blessed with little pain and full of intimacy. The garden has been both Gethsemane and Eden. I am at peace.

In the dawn I brew a first coffee with Sibelius rustling down the corridor. Later in the day HB is asleep – he always sleeps here with the TV on. Howard is in the garden, Phostrogening: 'Little and often, little and often.'

Wednesday evening

St Bartholomew's hospital

It makes me sad to be lying here with all these young men dying in the spring sunlight. The geriatrics have passed on, the HIV patients moved, exhausted, sick, trembling. I feel, recording this, that I am invading many private worlds, but I can't just sit helplessly – I have been given this gift. As they lie there, inert, my hand races across the page – many thousands of words a day. I've found that hospital is perfect for writing, at four or five in the morning. It's teatime now and I'm waiting for HB, who's bringing a string of pearls, then I'm off to the opera house with Howard. HB is also bringing *Christianity, Social Tolerance and Homosexuality* by John Boswell, which I will give to the hospital priests.

Meanwhile the young men die. Death stalks through the ward in this bright sunlight.

Opposite: At rear of cottage
Right: Wind-clipped rue

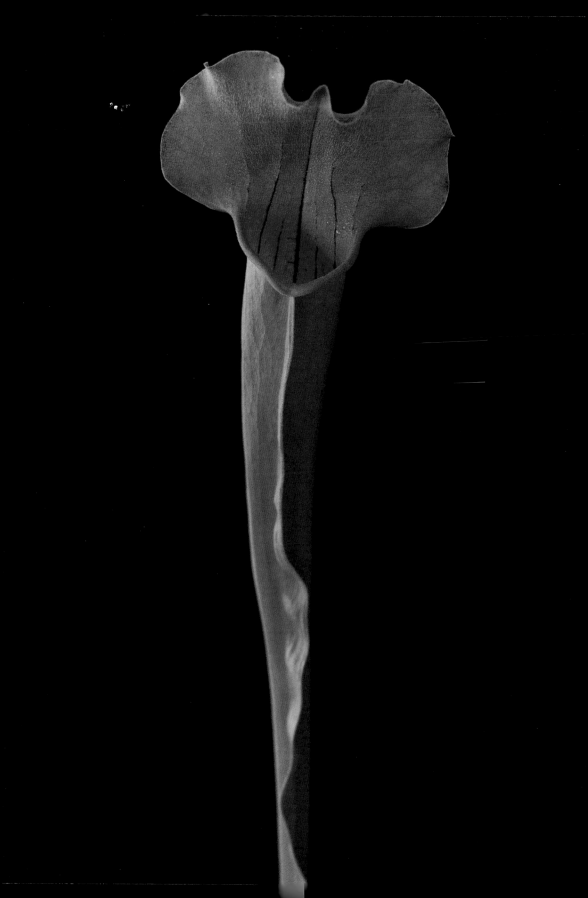

The lizards dance
in the santolina,
head over heels
in the Crambe maritima.
Fluffer is out on a prowl.
Like Thomas the cat
he stops and stares,
the lizards laugh as
they dance and play
loop the loop
under the sky
on this fine
sunny day.

Hinney Beast,
Hinney Beast,
Go away.

But Hinney Beast hovers
like the kestrel above,
Lizzy the lezzy lizard of love
— for lizards are curved,

not straight at all —
green and yellow they
scuttle away,
playing with Hinney Beast
all day long.

This is the lizards' Dungeness song:

Swing me high and sing me low,
bless us sun as we
bask in your glow,
give us a larder of flies for tea
and plenty of beetles
for lunch and as we
let the sun shine on
in the infinite blue
and Hinney Beast's
shadow — we can see you.

Hinney Beast
has
lost his shadow.

not short at all
green and yellow they
scuttle away.
Playing with honey bear
all day long

This is the Lizard
Dungeness song

Swing me high and swing
me low
bless us sun as we
bask in your glow
give us a tankard of   plenty
Flys for tea
and plenty of Bees
for lunch and tea as well
let the sun shine on
hi the infinite blue
and honey Bears
Shadow we can see you

honey Bears!
has no shadow

The lighthouse from the 1960s is an architectural wonder. The light turns every eleven seconds from a tall black and white tower which shoots up from a spiral.

The old lighthouse for tourists who cross the marsh on the Dungeness light railway has an extraordinary room of glass prisms – an Aladdin's cave. From the top you can see that the Ness is made of waves of shingle fanning out to the sea.

Above: Lens room in the lighthouse

Opposite: Facing the lighthouse

Hound's tongue, comfrey . . .

I particularly like the green and crimson
perennial pea. I can't understand why I haven't
introduced it into the garden. Perhaps it's an
acquired taste, for it has the look of a poisonous
plant – it looks dangerous. It's taken a bit of time
to take. The patch is about thirty feet long; it
doesn't grow anywhere else.

On Saturday, eight people could barely move
the huge baulk of timber from the beach, though
Karl brought it to Prospect end over end. We put it
in the circle of santolinas at the back. It's ten foot
high or more, part of an old ship.

Later, Howard planted Nottingham catchfly and
pea vetch which Joanna brought from the wild
flower nursery.

*Clockwise from top left: Derek
Ball, Peter Fillingham, Keith
Collins, Howard Sooley*

Below right: Kevin Collins

May 2

Bart's let me off the drip and Howard and I took
off to Dungeness. The day was grey when we set
out; we drove down the lanes in the shimmering
green of May. Time brings a uniformity to the
spectrum of green. Along the verges of the lane are
white ramsons, purple orchid, buttercup and
bluebell. Up hill, down dale we go to Prospect
Cottage, which grows like a tree – more beautiful
the older it becomes. The garden is fresh
and green as the lanes; it is filled with the flowers
of spring: some wonderful tulips: crimson and
yellow with a frill, and a deep purple one which
sways above the luxuriant tawny wallflowers, the
first white campion, blue-eyed forget-me-nots and
banks of marigolds; the *Crambe cordifolia* and
maritima are in bud, as are the Mrs Sinkins pinks.
The dragon-toothed rocks have almost disappeared,
the garden is off, the gun of spring fired.
The artichoke outside my window has fourteen
buds and is shoulder high, the huge thistles have
filled out, the roses are all in leaf, the sages are in
bud, the everlasting peas sprawl around lazily across
the shingle. The gorse, which took a battering, is
sprouting.

Cardoon

The garden is therapeutic in its peacefulness. Howard Phostrogened and planted the herbs we bought in Iden Croft Herbs: low growing thyme, tarragon, some pinks. We rooted out some double anemones – a flower destroyed by meddling – and put in a wine-black peony, and species elder and fennel around the cesspit.

At the side of the house the wooden sleeper squares look magnificent, filled with shingle. Peter is still cutting the poem 'Busie old foole, unruly Sunne' for the side of the house. I'm going to ask them to carry on here and build two *Crambe* squares and freshen the stones in the beds. I returned to Bart's happy, all my little tasks fulfilled.

Monet's garden at Giverny is an Edwardian garden of borders and gravel paths. Huge rose pergolas run riot. It is the shaggiest garden in the world, only possible to describe in the flecks and dabs of colour in his paintings. Although the white wisteria on the bridge was nearly over and the lilies not yet out, the main garden was a mass of irises, peonies and dew-laden roses.

It is such a contrast to the desert of Dungeness – rich, watery and sheltered behind its poplars. I doubt there is a plant that wouldn't thrive there.

In Monet's garden at Giverny

The scent of the Ness is gorse, though this can be overwhelmed by the sea, especially after a storm, when the seaweed snakes along the waterline.

On a hot day up beyond the power station where the purple iris and the bluebell grow, the heady, honeyed smell of the gorse can be almost too strong. The *Crambe maritima* also has a honeyed scent, so the entire Ness is honeyed. At this moment the tulips are out, with their sharp scent, and the Mrs Sinkins pinks and the dancing bouquets of wallflowers. After rain the resinous santolinas and sage are strong on the breeze – green santolina is the strongest. So my garden has the scent of the Garrigues, of warmth, and of the south.

Above: Poppies
Opposite: Marigold

The everlasting pea has little scent, neither do the
horehound and the Nottingham catchfly. Acrid
poppies make you sneeze and leave smudges of
black on the end of your nose. The dog rose has
a scent unlike other roses – less smooth, with a kick
in it. The foxgloves that march like soldiers in
platoons along the lake have a scent that is hardly
present at all.

The seaweed's back.

Foxgloves

Index

Acknowledgments

Thanks to: D. J. Hibberd, Axletree Nursery; Helen Ballard; Peter Beales, Peter Beales Roses; N. Stevens, Cambridge Bulbs; Joanna Westgate, Country Flowers Nursery; Christopher Lloyd, Great Dixter Nurseries; Bill Bradshaw, Greatstone Nursery; Rosemary and David Titterington, Iden Croft Herbs; Jacques Amand Ltd; Liam MacKenzie, Madrona Nursery; Alan C. Smith, The Sempervivum Society; Peter Moore, Tile Barn Nursery; Beth Chatto, Unusual Plants; Elizabeth Strangman and Graham Gough, Washfield Nursery.

The staff of St Andrewe's Ward, St Bartholomew's Hospital, and the staff of Wharfeside Clinic, St Mary's Hospital; Derek Ball; Brian Clarke; Julian Cole; Demetrios; Peter Fillingham; Lynn Hanke; HCHE; Nicholas Knightly; Catherine Lamb; Kevin Lawley; Steve and Denise Lilley; Karl Lydon; Tony Peake; David Pesher; Sarah Praill; John Richardson; Pat Rutland; Gary Scott; Brian Yale; Pop-it-in Pete and the Dungenettes.

The publishers would like to thank Keith Collins for his generous help in the preparation of this book.

wild flowers
sea pea
seakale
vipers Bugloss
horned yellow poppy
foxglove

yesternight I set out [...]
the fifth quarter of the [...]
coldest. the salt sea m[...]
the ocean gnaws at the sh[...]
to Nows wave like the He[...]
frosty this year. summ[...]
far distant. I on out [...]
innumerable stars white[...]
moonlight   I halte in [...]
shadows. cold giants walk b[...]